AUSTRALIAN POEMS THAT WOULD STUN A SHEEP

I was a teacher for thirty-six years with the Victorian Education Department, many of them as Headteacher of Rural Schools. I shifted to Tasmania with my wife in December 1993. I still do quite a bit of relief teaching in the Huon Valley.

My only previous publication is a novel, *Bess, the Black Orpington Swaggie* (ABC Books, 1993). This was also put out on tape by the ABC, and has been broadcast widely throughout Australia.

I broadcast regularly on the ABC's Sunday programme, where I tell stories of the old school-days, accompanying each talk with a poem I am the *Country Hour* poet for Tasmania's ABC Radio, on which I am broadcast weekly. I have just completed a thirty-episode serial, *Yendara*, which is due to go to air in December on nationwide ABC Regional Radio.

My wife, Yvonne, and I have four daughters (ages 19-25) and two young grandsons.

P.R.R.

To my wife and daughters, for their patient listening, positive criticism, and enthusiastic encouragement.

I also want to thank my daughter, Megan, for illustrating the cover and my daughter, Alana, for suggesting the title.

AUSTRALIAN POEMS THAT WOULD STUN A SHEEP

PHILIP R. RUSH

Published by
Philip R. Rush Pty. Ltd.
A.C.N. 082 969 882
224 Sunny Hills Road,
Glen Huon, Tas. 7109
Telephone: (03) 6266 6331
www.philiprush.com.au

Printed by
Flying Colours Printing
148 Invermay Road,
Invermay, Tas. 7248

Philip R. Rush, 1939-
Australian Poems That Would Stun A Sheep

ISBN 978 0 646 33939 9

1st printing 500 copies (October '95); 2nd printing 500 copies (November '95)
3rd printing 500 copies (January '96); 4th printing 500 copies (March '96)
5th printing 500 copies (April '96); 6th printing 1000 copies (May '96)
7th printing 1500 copies (July '96); 8th printing 1500 copies (September '96)
9th printing 2nd edition 2000 copies (Sep '97); 10th printing 2nd edition 2000 copies (April '98)
11th printing 2nd edition 2000 copies (Jan '99); 12th printing 2nd edition 2500 copies (Nov '99);
13th printing 2nd edition 2500 copies (Mar '01); 14th printing 2nd edition 2500 copies (Nov '02);
15th printing 2nd edition 2500 copies (Aug '07)

CONTENTS

THE JOYS OF FARMING

The cows have got mastitis, the calves are scourin' bad,
The dog has got arthritis, he's got it like me Dad!
The rooster's looking sickly, the hens refuse to lay,
The ferns are growing quickly, and I'm runnin' out of hay.
The fences all need strainin', the roof blew off me shed,
And now it's started rainin', and me wife is sick in bed.
The sheep will soon need shearin', three paddock gates are down,
The spoutin's all need cleanin' - the water's turnin' brown!
I need to use the harrows but one tractor tyre is flat,
And now some flamin' sparrow has just messed on me hat!
Me motor-cycle's busted, I think it's stripped a gear,
One water-tank has rusted, and me bull is lookin' queer!
The tax-man wants me money, the bank is on me back,
The door's near off the dunny,and the ducks have lost their quack!
And now I've started shakin', I'm shiverin' through and through;
All me joints are achin', I think I've caught the 'flu!

What's that I hear you speakin'? Talk louder, please, me lad!
The windmill's loudly creakin', and me hearin's goin' bad.
You ask why I'm complainin': you've got it wrong, my son,
I'm only just explainin' what's needin' to be done.
That's why autumn's quiet, there's not that much to do,
Come spring, it's near a riot! It's work the whole day through!

TO THE CATTLE FARMER

I was brought up in the city where a cow is just a cow,
And all I knew about them was they gave us milk, and how;
I also knew that beef was cattle well and truly dead,
And that was all the bovine knowledge stored within my head.

But I've lived now in the country for nigh on thirty years;
I've learnt that little bobby calves are not the same as steers;
And what's a springing heifer (not a cow that leaps a fence),
And that polled cattle have no horns to use in their defence.

I know the different breeds for beef - Red Poll and Murray Grey,
There's Devon too, and Hereford, and Belted Galloway,
Brahmin, Shorthorn, Angus, all are breeds we use for meat;
And, as for size, the Limousin is difficult to beat.

I know what's meant by drenching, and how to mark a calf;
(I thought it meant to catch it - and that raised many a laugh!)
And mastitis, brucellosis; leptospirosus too,
Are diseases found in cattle, not a Russian freighter's crew!

Not only beef, but dairy cattle I have learnt about;
The Friesian, Jersey, Guernsey, and the Ayrshire all stand out
As proven first-class milkers; and I shudder to recall
How, in my teenage arrogance, I thought I knew it all!

I thought the only breeds of cow were brown, or black and white;
I still remember how I spoke, and guessed that I was right:
"The black and white one's used for milk, the brown one's used for cream,"
My almost total ignorance would make a farmer scream!

But since that time I've learnt a lot, and still know but a part
Of all there is to know of beef and dairy farmer's art.
I take my hat off to you all, your skill is quite supreme;
(And, by the way, which are the cows which give us thickened cream?)

DAIRY FARMING IN WINTER

There's ice on the windows and frost on the ground,
A heavy white fog absorbs any sound;
The pipes are all frozen, the puddles are, too,
And the mud on the track has the texture of glue.
It's well before dawn that I yells for me dog,
But he's curled in a ball in his hollowed-out log.
Me motor-bike splutters, not liking the cold,
And neither do I, for I'm getting too old.
At last me bike's running, and that is the cue
For me dog to appear - he rides with me, too.
We look for the cows, they're down by the creek,
Miles from the shed when the weather is bleak!

I'm covered in mud as we slither and slide,
And I swear at the fog wishing I was inside!
The cows hear us coming, get up on their feet,
And Bluey, me heeler, then jumps off the seat.
Barking and snapping, he moves them along,
And I hear, in the distance, the plover's harsh song.
At last, in the gloom, the dairy I see,
And there is me son, standing, waiting for me.
"There's a cuppa here, Dad, and some sandwiches, too;
While you eat I'll begin to put some of them through."
By the time we have finished, the day has begun;
The fog's been dispersed by a watery sun.
We go back to a meal prepared by me wife,
Thinking how farming's a wonderful life!

HOW DOES A FARMER FILL IN HIS DAY?

We came to the city to take in a play,
And stopped at a pub for a meal on the way.
"Some blokes have it easy," I heard someone say.
"How does a farmer fill in his day?'

I rose from my seat, and then, face to face,
I decided to put this young bloke in his place.
"You ask how a farmer fills in his time;
I'll answer your question, and answer in rhyme."

"How does a farmer fill in his day?
Mostly, my son, it's work and no play,
I'm up every morning before it is light,
And often I'm working far into the night."

The chap interrupted, "Oh! Come off it, Blue;
You can't tell me a farmer's got that much to do."
The room became quiet, all eyes in the crowd,
Were looking at us as I started aloud.

"There's welding and digging,
And sawing and snigging,
And building and nailing,
And fencing and baling,
And cutting and lopping,
And pruning and cropping,
And picking and packing,
And raking and stacking,
And slashing and turning,
And stubble needs burning;
There's cleaning and humping,
And spraying and pumping,
And ploughing and tearing,
For soil needs preparing;

There's planting and stripping,
And herding and dipping,
Animals freighting,
Commodities crating;
There's milking and feeding,
And grooming and weeding,
And droving and drenching,
And marking and trenching,
And cleaning and clearing,
And sweeping and shearing,
And drafting and mixing,
And greasing and fixing.
There's hoeing and sowing and mowing and showing,
And mending and wending and sending and tending.
There's draining and straining, and dogs that need training;
Furrowing, harvesting, marketing, harrowing,
Mustering, hammering, sharpening, barrowing.
Fertilising, merchandising, irrigating, cultivating,
Immunising, fumigating, separating, operating."

I paused; and the folk in the room all applauded,
And my answer, in rhyme, was duly rewarded;
For the chap spoke again, "I'll buy you a drink;
You've more than answered my question, I think!"

THE FARMER'S WIFE

Make the beds and cut the lunches,
Get the washing on the line;
Stop the kids from throwing punches,
See they reach the school on time.
To the woodshed, do some chopping,
Fill the wood-box, light the fire;
Drive to town and do the shopping,
Got a puncture - change the tire!
Pick a part up for the baler,
And a fan-belt for the ute,
Load the calf-feed in the trailer,
And the stuff to spray the fruit.
Wait in line to do the banking,
Listen to a neighbour grump.
Buy some oil to stop the clanking
In the fire-fighting pump.
Drive back home and start unpacking,
Clear the mess that's on the seat;
Through the door her husband's tracking,
Stop for half-an-hour to eat.
By the shed the calves need feeding,
Judging by their cries intense,
Feed the calves, and do some weeding,
Then help strain the sagging fence.
Still some time, so slash the bracken
Before returning to the house,
Still her pace she doesn't slacken,
The farmer's most proficient spouse.
In the kitchen, meal-preparing,
From the teapot pour a cup;
Then it's to the school repairing,
Time to pick the children up.
Listen to "Three Golden Wishes,"
(That's David's book that must be read;)
Clear the kitchen, wash the dishes,
See the children off to bed.
House and farm accounts need doing,
Work on them an hour or so;
Do some television viewing,
Then it's off to bed she goes.

How on earth does she keep going,
Living such a hectic life,
But this busy to and fro-ing,
Is normal for the farmer's wife.
Few there are who sing her praises,
Or about her ever tell.
I, for one, a cheer raises,
For the job she does so well.

THE OLD BEDFORD TRUCK

The old Bedford truck has been with us for years,
We've used it for sheep, and we've used it for steers;
And we've used it, of course, as a flat-bottomed tray
For the last twenty years when carting the hay.

Fence-posts and droppers, rolls of barbed wire,
Machinery parts, and the odd tractor tyre;
Sacks of potatoes, calf-feed and grain,
The Bedford has carried again and again.

The windscreen is cracked, the upholstery's gone,
There's a sack on the seat that the driver sits on.
The red paint on the truck, once shiny and new,
Is faded and worn, and the rust's showing through.

There's a dint here and there, and the windows don't wind;
The speedo don't work, but nobody minds.
The wood on the tray is twisted and split,
And the crate we once used, these days doesn't fit.

The cabin is draughty, there's holes in the floor,
You can't even open the passenger door!
The diff's got a rattle, the pedals are bare;
And the glass in the headlights is not even there!

The engine's not bad, most days it'll run,
So long as it's stood for a while in the sun.
It's still good for years, with some sort of luck;
For I'd hate to get rid of me old Bedford truck.

ACCIDENT PRONE

I'd heard about blokes who were accident prone,
But no-one like that had I personally known,
Until last December when Mike came to stay,
And offered to help on the farm every day.

In summer we're busy, you know what it's like,
And so I accepted this offer from Mike;
We'd hay to get in, and some fencing to do,
Drenching and milking, and wood-chopping, too.

First morning Mike helped me to load up the ute,
And managed to drop a post on me boot!
It landed so hard me toes all went numb,
And then, shutting the door, he jammed me left thumb!

We started some fencing, Mike picked up the maul,
While I held the post, otherwise it'd fall;
Mike swung the hammer, but missed, and hit me,
I thought, for a moment, he'd shattered me knee!

I said, "Leave the post; the barbed wire needs a strain,"
And that's what he did, but I cannot explain
How he somehow let go, and it wrapped round me shirt,
Tearing me flesh, and, boy! did it hurt!

I decided the fence could be left for a bit,
And I showed Mike some wood that we needed to split;
"No problems," he grinned; I walked t'wards the shed,
When the axe cracked me shoulder, me neck, and me head!

"Sorry," Mike called. "It just flew from me hand!"
I muttered some words as I struggled to stand,
"From now on, young chap, you can work on your own,
You're a danger to me, for you're accident-prone!"

A HEALTHY LIFESTYLE

They tell me farming's healthy, and maybe you agree,
But I can tell you squarely that it's not been kind to me.
Not that I'm complainin', I've had a decent life,
But farming's caused me body a fair amount of strife.

I suffer from arthritis, and rheumatism, too,
And, every flamin' winter, I catch the wretched 'flu;
Me hips are not too handy, me right knee's pretty crook,
High-tensile took me eye out so I've got a one-eyed look.

Through carting hay and timber I've jiggered up me back,
And, every time I twist me neck, I hear a nasty crack;
Me ticker's not too bad, I guess, I have a murmur there,
And, prob'ly due to worry, I've lost me head of hair.

I've got a lot of spots and things through being in the sun,
Each time I see the doctor he removes another one;
Me left hand isn't pretty, I crushed it years ago,
And, when splitting up some fence-posts, I lost me second toe.

I don't get quite so breathless since I've given up the smokes,
But I don't think I'm as healthy as all you other folks,
But still I work eight hours a day, thankful I'm alive,
Which isn't bad, I reckon, for a bloke who's ninety-five!

THE HAY SHED

It was built by me dad in the early years with a bit of help from his mate,
And stands in the paddock behind the house, a little uphill of the gate.
It's a sturdy shed, and a good size too; three thousand bales and more
We've managed to pack beneath its roof - when we've had that much to store.

The iron roof has a bit of rust, and it leans a bit to the east;
The wind 'round here blows most from the west, annoyin' both man and beast.
It's not the handsomest shed around, and it's years since it was new;
You can see the scars on the ironbark posts from the fires of sixty-two.

The cattle and sheep are kept at bay by a makeshift barbed wire fence;
We had in mind to replace it, but that don't make no sense:
Dad built it temp'ry, after the fire, for the first one burnt to the ground,
But, apart from a rotten post or two, it still looks pretty sound.

A couple o' cats live up in the hay, they rarely come to the house;
For there's shelter there, and comfort, too, and always a feed of mouse.
We like 'em there, for mice are a plague,and they keep their numbers down;
And we've managed to give the kittens away to people who live in town.

There's not much else I've got to add, what can you say of a shed?
You should have asked me to tell you about me stock or crops instead.
But you asked 'bout the shed, the old hay shed, the one over there on the hill;
And it wouldn't surprise, when I'm dead and gone, that the shed'll be standing still!

BALER TWINE

The gate's tied up with baler twine,
And so is the dairy door;
And I've used the same for the "HAZCHEM" sign
That I have to display, by law.
And I use it, too, when I drive the ute,
It keeps the dog on the tray.
The lace disappeared from me leather boot,
So I've laced it with twine today.
The tomato plants are firmly tied
To their stakes, and the dahlias too,
By some baler twine - and around the side
It's helping support the flue.
It keeps me trousers from falling down
As I'm working around the place:
But I wears me belt when I goes to town,
Or me wife says I look a disgrace!
I use this wonderful baler twine
Dozens of times every day;
I even use this string so fine
To tie up the bales of hay!

MY OLD ENAMEL MUG

I've drunk from Royal Doulton and from Royal Albert too;
I've drunk from classic Wedgwood from a cup of white and blue;
I've drunk from Irish Porcelain, and from a Pyrex jug;
But billy tea tastes best when drunk from my enamel mug.

I've had my old enamel mug since nineteen forty-six;
I've used it in the city, and way up in the sticks;
From Melbourne town to Flinders Range, from Brisbane to Taree;
I've used my old enamel mug to hold my billy tea.

The white enamel's somewhat stained and has a dozen chips;
And when the tea is piping hot, the blue rim burns my lips;
But when working in the paddock, cutting wood, or carting hay,
My friend, the old enamel mug, is never far away.

So when I'm in the mountains, on the plain, or by the sea;
When I'm picnicking with others, or when there's only me,
I'll boil the blackened billy, and sit by the campfire snug,
For tea tastes best when drinking from my old enamel mug.

THE GATE

For forty-five years the gate had kept the stock from the nearby road;
It had served the farmer faithfully through seasons that ebbed and flowed
Like tides on the ocean beaches, it had never been known to fail;
It stood, whatever the weather, in the rain and the snow and the hail.

It wasn't one of them fancy gates made of mesh and tubular pipe;
It was built to an old and tried design, not one of your modern type.
It was made of wood; it had five long rails, and a stay to keep them straight,
But the stay had long since broken; it had yielded under the weight.

The timber rails were weathered and worn; their colour had turned to grey;
They were bent and bowed through years of use, and were wired to the broken stay.
The nails that had once been shiny and bright were pretty well rusted through,
And the iron that was nailed to the bottom was badly rusted too.

The lower hinge had long since gone, and the one at the top was bent;
The catch was lost, just disappeared! No-one knew where it went;
So the gate was shut with baler twine tied round the strainer post;
And the farmer cursed every time he came, for he used that gate the most!

And then, one day, when he opened the gate, it crashed to the ground with a thud;
And the farmer swore as he found himself bespattered all over with mud.
He threw the gate on his well-used ute, and it overhung the back;
And, when he returned to the house for lunch, he tossed it onto the stack.

He replaced the gate with a "Weldmesh" one; it took him an hour or two;
And it did the job that he wanted, for none of the stock got through.
He drove back home, and his wife came out. "The bull has escaped," she said.
"He smashed the gate and has cornered a cow behind the machinery shed."

With the help of his dog he shifted the bull well away from the rest of the stock,
To a paddock girt with a seven-wire fence, the most secure on his block.
He returned to the gate the bull had smashed; it was damaged beyond repair,
And he had nought else to replace it, and his wife then heard him swear.

She called, in a tone most gentle, so as not to annoy him more,
"There's an old gate here," and she showed him what he'd tossed on the stack before.
It didn't get burned, as he meant it to; it has pride of place instead,
Still serving the farmer faithfully, beside the machinery shed.

THE HAYSTACK

With thunderstorms at evening, and century heat each day,
The weather was appalling, but still we carted hay:
We stacked it in the paddock, and worked while it was light,
And took a largish trailer-load home with us each night.

The paddocks we were cutting were fifteen miles from home,
Down towards the ocean on a light and sandy loam;
And the bales we carted homeward, although the hour was late,
We unloaded near the dairy, beside the paddock gate.

The bales had been rained upon, and so were pretty wet,
And we salted every layer, for we knew how hot they'd get
If we left them all untreated: and the stack grew every night;
Three thousand bales or more it had - a most impressive sight.

When we reached a dozen high we let the salting stop.
And finished off our haystack with a pitched roof at the top.
Grandpa made a cover with a hundred bags or so,
And said, "The stack reminds me of a little church I know."

Me mate suggested I could preach from there on Sunday next,
And said that "Love your neighbour" might make a goodish text.
I said, that if he listened, I'd preach there every day,
He spluttered in his coffee, uncertain what to say.

It wasn't that much later - a month, or maybe two,
We were sitting in the garden, for the day was nearly through;
When we noticed from the haystack there came a cloud of smoke,
And we raced toward the dairy, along with other folk.

We saved the sheds and fences, and other things around,
But our well-constructed haystack burnt completely to the ground.
'Spontaneously combusted' - that's what the firemen said;
So I had to do me preaching from some other place instead!

ROLL BARS

I've got a mate whose farm includes a steepish bit of land,
A thirty-acre paddock, partly cleared;
But when we talked of danger he'd dismiss it out of hand,
No tractor-tipping accident he feared!

He'd feed his cows a bit of hay, or pull the harrows round,
And sometimes give a rotten stump a push;
His wife was always anxious when he worked that bit of ground,
Or logged inside their little patch of bush.

But she, herself, would sometimes drive the tractor up there, too,
Feeling safe because she took a little care.
She liked to slash the bracken, which interminably grew
Throughout the district almost everywhere!

One day she came to see us (which she often used to do,
And join us in a cuppa and a talk);
But this time she was miserable; her legs were black and blue,
She found it quite an effort just to walk!

She had other massive bruises, and she ached from head to toe,
But she was thankful just to be alive,
She'd been slashing with the tractor, and only driving slow,
When she hit a stump and took a nasty dive.

The tractor didn't crush her,but it tipped her off the seat,
And slowly settled back upon its wheels;
She said, "I thought I'd had it, my death about to meet,
Now I know how vulnerable one feels."

Our friend has quite recovered, and she drives the tractor still,
Even on that steepish bit of land;
But the tractor now has roll-bars, to protect her on the hill;
All tractors without roll-bars should be banned!

ROCK WALLS

All over our block
We've a jumble of rock,
And I, with unending endeavour,
Am shifting those stones,
With a creaking of bones,
To make walls exceedingly clever.

I've not spent a cent
On sand or cement;
For I have been doing dry-walling.
And, since they still stand
And look rather grand,
Maybe I've discovered my calling!

THE WHEAT TRAIN

The Wimmera wheat
In the blazing heat
Had ripened and turned to gold:
And the farmers' glee
Was easy to see
As amongst their crops they strolled.
The northerly breeze
Brought a hundred degrees,
And the farmers looked to their sheds.
Soon the tractors roared
Through the paddocks broad
As they gathered the golden heads.
From the morning light,
Through the summer's night,
The harvesters worked their best.
While the weather held
There was no-one spelled,
Except for a few hours rest.
As the paddock bins
Were filled, so the grins
On the farmers' faces stretched.
Soon on dusty roads
There were many loads
Of wheat to the railways fetched.
After being weighed,
And delivery made
Into silos standing tall;
Back to gathered grain
Raced the trucks again
To finish their golden haul.
As the silos filled,
So the workers milled
Around engine, wagon, and truck;
And the railway crews
Checked the bolts and screws,
For nothing was left to luck.
Then in fiercesome heat
Trucks were filled with wheat
And hooked to the engines strong:
And the dusty train

Left the station again
With a load a half-mile long.
And the clickety-clack
Of the train on track
Was heard from many a bed:
And it seemed to say
The wheat's on its way
To becoming your daily bread.

RED

Red is the sky on a hot summer's night,
Red is the Hereford's coat;
Red is the colour of autumn's delight,
Red is a twenty-buck note.

Red is the soil at the foot of the mount;
Red is the heath in the scrub.
Red is the drought-ridden farmer's account,
Red is the wine in the tub.

Red is the kelpie that rounds up the sheep,
Red is the roof on the shed.
Red is the eye that does nothing but weep;
Red is the heart that has bled.

Red is the nose on a cold winter's day,
Red is the glow of the fire;
Red are the faces of children at play;
Red are the cheeks of the liar.

Red is the comb on the rooster and hen,
Red are the apples full-grown;
Red is a robin. And red is the pen
Of most of the teachers I've known.

Red is for Christmas, and red is for flame;
Red is the old Bedford truck,
And, for all the people who like a good game,
Red is the colour of luck.

THE SHEARING SHED

I was standing in the shearing shed with no one else around;
A door swung idly in the breeze - there was no other sound.
Two bales of crutchings lay nearby; and half a bale, or less,
Of skirtings lay untidily beside the silent press.

The classing table with its slats was up against the wall;
The shearing plants with no handpiece could do no work at all.
The smell was there, but not the same without the restless sheep,
And e'en the bats beneath the roof hung quietly, fast asleep.

A billy sat upon a shelf beside a broken cup;
And, way off in the distance, I heard a yelping pup.
The barking seemed to bring alive the sleeping shearing shed,
And thoughts and dreams of shearers past and old sheds filled my head.

My mind went back near fifty years to when, as just a lad,
I saw my first large shearing shed - two score of stands it had.
I dreamt I was a shearing gun, and in my dreams I saw
That I could shear three hundred sheep, and some days even more.

I saw the ghost of Jackie Howe; I heard the clanging bell;
I heard the noise of whirring shafts; I heard the angry yell
Of "sheep-o!" as a pen was found as empty as could be;
And then my dream was broken by "Let's have a cup of tea!"

DROUGHT

It's dry!
The country's dry, for sure it is, we've had no decent rains
For years up on the Tablelands, or on the Western Plains.
Why! Even Tassie's gripped by drought - most Midland dams are dry,
And daily farmers vainly search the unproductive sky.

The wheat crop's going to fail again, it hasn't had a chance;
The hundred acre paddocks now are just a bare expanse.
And feed is short for beef and sheep, if feed is there at all,
And few there are still living can as bad a drought recall.

Oh! it was bad in forty-four, when red dust filled the skies,
And nineteen two and three were crook, but this one takes the prize.
There's some away out west, they say, have gone for ten years now,
With less than average rainfall, but they're hanging on, somehow.

They say it's got to rain again, I guess that's true enough,
But, 'til that day, I tell you, lad, we're going to do it tough;
And, even then, we're looking at a long and weary road
Before our ten long years of debt will loose its crushing load.

It's dry!
On many farms the breeding stock is all that now remains
Of massive mobs of sheep and beef, and only decent rains
Will give the farmer any hope of building up his herd
To something like the size he had before this drought occurred.

It's dry!
Not just the dams and creeks are dry, our souls are parched as well,
Drained by anxiety and debt, sapped by this long dry spell.
But we're a hard and sturdy lot, we'll see this cruel drought through,
For rain will come to bring alive our hopes, and pastures, too.

RABBITS

Rabbits, rabbits everywhere, such a flamin' pest;
For years these wretched creatures have put me to the test!
They eat up all me pasture, they undermine the fence,
And me efforts to get rid of them has caused me great expense.

I started, as a youngster, setting fifty traps and more,
I'd set them in the morning and catch rabbits by the score;
I sold them to some joker for sixpence every pair,
But, regardless of me trapping, we had rabbits everywhere.

Next we bought some ferrets, and half a dozen nets,
The ferrets were attractive, and made pretty decent pets;
But our rabbit population continued to increase,
So we chose to let our ferreting and rabbit-trapping cease.

We tried smoking out the rabbits, and fumigating, too;
But the burrows seemed deserted, as if the rabbits knew.
We ripped up every warren that we found around the place,
And fired, with our rifles, at every bunny face.

When myxo came to Tassie, it slowed 'em up a bit;
But the rabbit wasn't beaten, and they all refused to quit;
They bred a super rabbit that resists the myxo strain,
And now our grassy paddocks are full of them again.

I'm not keen on ten-eighty, or any sort of bait,
For a variety of reasons, but I'll not elaborate;
If we had a growing market for rabbit skins and meat,
I'd take up rabbit-farming and get rid of all me sheep!

MY HAT

I've bought a new Akubra but it's not yet broken in,
It still feels stiff and solid and sits harshly on my skin.
The old one's stained and battered, but it's easy on my head,
So soft that when I'm camping it's the pillow on my bed.

The new hat looks pretentious, sort of shouts at passers-by;
And the rim's so hard and rigid it could damage someone's eye!
But the old hat's worn and faded with a self-effacing air,
And its softened felt and leather makes it comfortable to wear.

My hat is uncomplaining, it's a trusted loyal friend;
We've been partners now for years, and I don't want this to end.
In every kind of weather; in the heat, or rain, or hail,
My hat has proved its value, it's never been known to fail.

So why buy a new Akubra? you well may ask of me;
My wife supplied the answer, and my daughters all agree.
"That hat is quite disgusting," and she added, with some force,
"If you wear that hat in public, it may lead to a divorce!"

THE POST AND RAIL FENCE

Electric fences are common as mud,
And no use at all if the battery's a dud.
If you needed a fence that was sure not to fail,
You couldn't improve on the old post and rail.

Nowadays on our farms when fencing is done,
Star posts and steel droppers are given a run.
This fence may be fine, but in character pale
Compared with the look of the old post and rail.

A modern day fence with high tensile wire
Is not one that people will stop and admire;
But many a tourist in sun, rain, or hail,
Stops and takes snaps of the old post and rail.

Ringlock and weldmesh, cyclone and net,
Are some of the fences I've recently met.
But none have the charm, on hilltop or dale,
Like the fence now uncommon, the old post and rail.

MY CHAINSAW

My chainsaw has died;
Bruce said that it would.
On it I relied
To cut all my wood.

It ran very well
For twelve years or so;
Then, I'm sorry to tell,
It let its age show.

Its breath became short,
And a cold or the 'flu
Every winter it caught
Until 'ninety-two.

In August that year
It hiccoughed a bit;
Then, with clatterings queer,
It suffered a fit!

I took it to Bruce
Who, since 'seventy-six,
Its behaviour obtuse
Had managed to fix.

This spluttering saw
He tried to repair;
He'd told me before
To treat it with care.

I went back at ten
O'clock the next day;
And Bruce told me then
To throw it away.

"I'm telling you, son,
It's leaving life's stage,
It's finished its run;
It's died of old age."

I'm off to the store,
A thousand to spend,
To buy a new saw
To replace an old friend.

DISEASE FREE

My wife helped Bill inject his lambs
One Friday afternoon;
He'd moved them from the ewes and rams
That he'd be shearing soon.

Bill had asked my wife to help
Because she was a nurse;

She'd rarely made a patient yelp,
But lambs were more perverse.

Each lamb that she'd injected was
From pulpy kidney saved:
But Bill became annoyed because
They often misbehaved.

He'd lift each lamb and hold it tight
As she the needle used;
But many fought and kicked in fright
At being so abused.

Eight hundred lambs were done, which meant
Just fifty more at most:
But Bill was tiring fast; he leant
Upon a nearby post.

His aching back he bent again
Another lamb to fetch:
The one he caught was "raising Cain",
A struggling little wretch!

My wife, with needle poised to plunge
Into the woolly shape,
Was distracted by the sudden lunge
The lamb made to escape.

Bill released this lamb he'd grabbed;
But worse was yet to come;
The needle with the vaccine stabbed
Into the poor man's thumb!

Pain made Bill's facial features crease,
But of one thing he's sure:
Pulpy kidney's one disease
He's free from evermore!

CITY VERSUS COUNTRY

When you live down in the city
Where the air is grey and gritty;
And the scenery's not pretty
When compared with country views;
It's all run and rush and bustle,
As the people have to tussle
With the frantic city's hustle
And the never-ending queues.

And there's traffic! traffic! traffic!
Nothing stops and nothing's static;
Sirens blaring, horns emphatic,
Can be heard both day and night.
Trams and trains and buses roaring,
Trucks, all traffic rules ignoring,
As they make their way full-boring,
Looking not to left or right!

And there's really no containment
Of this haste, e'en entertainment,
With its payment! payment! payment!
Is pursued at breathless pace.
Whether discotheque or ballet,
Movie, play, or sideshow alley,
Or a concert at the Palais;
It's all noise and crowds and race.

And the precious times of leisure,
Which the city dwellers treasure,
Are devoid of simple pleasure
In the crowded urban scene.
For at weekends round our nation,
All the city population
Seek for sim'lar destinations,
Hence no hope of peace serene.

But here in the country it isn't the same,
And perhaps, to the townie, it's all rather tame;
But me - I'm glad to the country I came
And took up my residence here,

The noise of the city, the frenzy, the haste,
Up here in the country by peace is replaced;
And the air that surrounds you has no grimy taste,
It's fresh, unpolluted, and clear.

There's time to relax and chat to a friend;
Our lives are not governed by fashion or trend.
And hours in the traffic you don't have to spend;
Our days seem to be a lot freer.

There may be a moral, or may be there's not;
But some think I came to the country to rot;
But the pace of the city don't suit me one jot;
I'll stay, in contentment, right here!

WEEDS

Barley Grass, Canary Grass, Cocksfoot, and Sedge,
Box Thorn and Blackberry as thick as any hedge;
Capeweed, Pigweed, Wild Oat and Flax,
And Sweet Briar so thick I need a flamin' axe!

Burdock and Foxtail, Onion Weed and Gorse,
Pampas Grass and Hoary Cress, and Bindweed, of course.
Chickweed and Fat Hen, and Three-cornered Jack,
Soursob and Stinkweed, and Nightshade Black.

Dandelion and Groundsel, Ribwort and Burr,
And there's hardly any places where thistles don't occur!
Kikuyu and Wireweed, Curled and Fiddle Dock,
And Ragwort and Bracken, both bad for stock.

Weeds! Weeds! Weeds! Weeds! Everywhere I look;
There's so many weeds here, they'd fill a flamin' book!
Where they all came from I guess I'll never know,
But, if they could hear me, I'd tell them where to go!

COUNTRY MUSIC

I heard him on the radio, some educated bloke,
Talking country music: to me it seemed a joke
That someone from the city should tell us rural folk
What all this country music is about.

He spoke of Kernegan, I think, and Williamson, and Brooks;
And Johnny Cash he mentioned, with his weatherbeaten looks;
And he said that our Slim Dusty is in all the record books,
For the great amount of albums he's put out.

I suppose that all these singers deserve their bit of fame,
As do many others that this chap went on to name,
Who've each become an item in the country singing game,
They've all worked hard to reach the top, no doubt.

I'll admit I sometimes listen to these country music stars,
I've even sung along with them for half a dozen bars,
As they grumble out the lyrics and strum their swank guitars,
Encouraging their fans to scream and shout.

But there is a better music in this countryside of ours,
You'll hear it in the breezes, and the lowing of the cows,
In the piping songs of robins, and the ravens' mournful howls,
And the morning splash of early-rising trout.

You'll hear it in the mountains, and on the rolling plain.
You'll hear it on the iron roof, as gently-falling rain
Sweetly sings its music and adds its own refrain,
As it hurries down a metal waterspout.

You'll hear it in the thunder as it rolls around the hills,
And in the mighty rivers, and the many tinkling rills,
You'll hear it in the magpie and the sombre thrush's trills;
That's what country music's all about.

ON ANZAC DAY

Down the years the storms of strife have rarely crossed our native shore,
But winds from lands beyond the seas have brought with them the stench of war.
Revenge and envy, greed and hate, a lust for dominance and power;
And threatened nations far and wide have called for help in desperate hour.

Unprepared to stand aside, to watch our friends and allies fall,
And wishing to protect the peace that is the privilege of us all;
The men and women of our land, from office, factory, shop and farm,
Have volunteered to fight for right, and keep our families free from harm.

Exchanging tractors, ploughs and trucks, for bayonets, guns and armoured tanks,
Our farmers willingly have fought, and earned our everlasting thanks.
Leaving pastures green behind, and paddocks full of golden wheat,
And, giving all, have bled and died, with foreign soil beneath their feet.

In countries all around the globe, Vietnam, France and Singapore,
New Guinea, Egypt, and Korea, in Palestine and many more;
Australians served our country well, and many families suffered loss,
Those who returned have left behind their mates beneath a simple cross.

The fallen didn't die in vain, our land and people still are free,
And they died, not for themselves, they died for you, and died for me.
We remember them with pride, and from our hearts we humbly say
Our prayers of gratitude for them, on this Australia's Anzac Day.

LANDCARE

We cut down the gum-trees, we pulled out the stumps,
We ploughed in the grasses, and levelled the bumps;
Any scrub that remained we burnt in a pile,
And our work was admired, at least, for a while.

From the trunks of the trees we cut many posts,
And fenced in the land from the hills to the coast,

The paddocks created we harrowed and sowed,
And were all quite delighted when new pasture showed.

We fattened the cattle, we raised many lambs,
From the sleekest of pigs we smoked beautiful hams.
Lucerne and barley, potatoes and peas,
We grew in the paddocks where once there were trees.

'Though good for a while, 'twas not very long
That things on our farms went drastically wrong.
Erosion was rife, and the wind blew away
Much of the soil into ocean and bay.

And the earth that was left wasn't nearly as good,
It wouldn't grow pastures as well as it should;
Fertiliser we used to give it a hand,
But we still weren't getting the best from our land.

Generations have gone since our farms were begun,
And many we've handed from father to son;
Well over a century of wear and abuse,
And some of our land is of now little use.

But all is not lost, we're trying to redeem
The soil blown away, or eroded by stream.
We're replanting trees, and trying to repair,
Our degenerate land with cooperative care.

THE SHOW

I'm at the Show with all its stalls,
The moving clowns and ping-pong balls;
The lucky dips, the gaudy toys,
Attracting lots of girls and boys.
The doughnut, chips, and hot-dog stands
That leave us all with greasy hands.
The ferris wheels, and spinning rides
That tend to trouble my insides!

And here I can make little sense
Of calls of spruikers by their tents,
Their voices garbled or distorted
By microphones in hands supported.
Out in the main arena, too,
Loudspeakers shout at all in view,
Announcing which event is on,
And winners in the one just gone.

But I like animals the best,
I could do without the rest.
The horses, goats - the cocks and hens,
Enormous pigs in concrete pens,
Soft-eyed cows and massive bulls,
Sheep displayed with finest wools;
The choicest animals to see,
That's what the Show is meant to be.

THE DESERTED FARMHOUSE

The iron roof has a rusty tinge,
The chimney's worn and cracked,
The front door hangs from a single hinge,
No window-pane's intact.

The greying timbers, bare and bleak,
Have lost all sign of paint,
The floorboards give a weary creak,
Beneath our footfall faint.

The papered walls are faded brown,
Musty, stained, and torn.
Thick cobwebs, wraithlike, hanging down,
Augment this scene forlorn.

A portrait hangs from the picture rail,
Dulled by the passing years;
A sign, held up by a rusty nail,
Reads dim, "The cup that cheers."

The yard outside is dismal too,
Most of the garden's dead;
A single rosebush struggles through
The blackberries by the shed.

A hundred years the house had been
A warm and vibrant home;
But now,deserted, stands unseen
At evening, in the gloam.

It has no lived-in look today,
The family now has gone.
And, slowly eaten by decay,
Their house will too, pass on.

THE BULLDOG TRACTOR

Single cylinder Bulldogs,
Throbbing through the day;
Back in the nineteen forties,
They were here to stay:
Thump! Thump! Thump!

On many a farm and station
They were a vital part.
Now they're obsolescent,
Like the horse and cart.
Thump! Thump! Thump!

The Bulldog had a glowplug
You had to heat a lot;
So farmers used a blowtorch
To make the glowplug hot.
Thump! Thump! Thump!

Once the plug was heated,
The flywheel then was turned
Until the engine started,
And the diesel burned.
Thump! Thump! Thump!

Now the Bulldog tractor
Is part of yesteryear;
And its steady throbbing
Is but a memory dear.
Thump! Thump!Thump!

THE FURPHY FARM WATER CART

Set on a trailer of metal and wood, with a large iron wheel on each flank,
The redoubtable Furphy was known country-wide, the ubiquitous farm water tank.
They came in a range of sizes and shapes, and one you're still likely to see,
Is the hundred gallon capacity one, the tank most appealing to me.

A galvanised cylinder set on its side with a cast iron plate at each end;
The lid at the top was cast iron too, and therefore unlikely to bend.
The tap at the back was of useful design, with a large diameter pipe,
And the part you attached to the tractor was a utilitarian type.

The makers were Furphy's, from Shepparton Town, and written on each iron plate
Was a list of their products, like plough wheels and troughs; steel shares, and an excellent gate.
They also made horse-works, whatever that meant, and something they called swingle-trees;
(I looked up a book to find out what it was, for the word was a new one to me.)

A centrally-pivotting bar it was, and the traces of each pulling horse
Were attached to each end of a swingle-tree; well before my time, of course!
But when the name "Furphy" is spoken about, most farmers will straightway recall
Furphy's remarkable farm water cart, their most famous product of all!

TRUST

It's not like me to have me doubts, I always trust a bloke,
Although I must admit, at times, I've had me little joke.
And played a trick, or maybe two, on unsuspecting mates,
But not again; I think I know what now a fella hates.
I won't again make fun of them, or put them ill at ease,
"It isn't right," we tell our kids, "to bully or to tease;
Or play a joke that makes us laugh at some poor kid's expense,
Especially when he has no friends to come to his defence."
And, though I like me little jokes, no more will I offend,
For I've discovered what it's like on the receiving end.

THE FARMERS' UNIFORM

When I visit my bank I note that the staff are dressed in a uniform way,
And so are the folk who work in the shop where I buy my supplies every day.
The Post Office people are uniformed too, and so are the local police,
As are the mechanics who work on my car, their outfits all covered in grease!

But what about farmers? Do they have a rig that sets them apart from the rest?
A jacket, perhaps, with its own special colours, or, maybe, a fancy-type vest?
It's hard to imagine our farmers in costume; but yet, I feel I can say,
Farmers do have a uniform too, at least in a vague sort of way.

I'll start from the bottom; there's black rubber gum-boots, for working when mud is about;
Or strong leather boots with sides of elastic, from Blundstones or Williams, no doubt.
For trousers there's moleskins for formal attire: for working there's Yakka's or jeans,
And solid-hide belts to keep them from falling, and a knife-pouch can often be seen.

A navy-blue singlet was once an essential, but now it is optional dress.
The flannelette shirt is still highly favoured, the checked ones most common, I guess.

And then, in the winter, an old woollen jumper, with holes where the elbows should be,
And, over the lot, a comfy old sports coat, or a waterproof mac to the knee.

And then there's the hat, the piece de resistance, slightly askew it is worn,
With the brim turned down at the front and the rear, the crown all battered and torn;
The hat should be faded and slightly discoloured, with string used to sew up each tear,
And that, my dear friends, completes the description of the uniform good farmers wear.

CHRISTMAS

It's been a hard year, of that there's no doubt,
For much of the country is suffering drought.
Wool prices have risen, but not yet enough,
And life for the woolgrower's still pretty tough.
The wheat cockie's struggling; without any rain
There isn't a chance he'll be harvesting grain.
The cotton crop's weaker, our beef herds are down,
The downturn in farming's hurt many a town.
Lamb prices are lower than this time last year,

And water restrictions are spreading, I fear.
Just when you're wondering how you will cope,
Christmas approaches, and Christmas brings hope.
When friends and when families gather each year,
The season of giving, the season of cheer.
The time to be thankful our land is at peace
In a world where wars only seem to increase.
Be thankful for food that we have on our table,
Be thankful if one is both healthy and able.
The season when all can look forward, and know
That rains will return and the pastures will grow;
The time to remember the manger and stall,
And a time to say Merry Christmas to all.

THE HUON AGRICULTURAL SOCIETY'S 48th HUON SHOW

Having lived in the Huon for nearly a year, we thought it was proper to go
To the Huon Agricultural Society's Do, their forty-eighth Annual Show.
After eating our lunch we drove in our car to Ranelagh, where it was at,
I was dressed for the part, with my moleskins and boots, a checked cotton shirt and my hat.

I expected to park in the Showground itself, or at least somewhere close to the gate,
But the Showground was packed, and so were the roads; we should have gone early, not late!
After parking the car half a mile from the Show in the first vacant spot that I found,
We put on our coats, locked the doors of the car, and wandered along to the ground.

We thought that an hour, or, at the most, two, would give us more time than enough,
To see all the stalls, the animals too, agricultural and hand-crafted stuff.
But oh! we were wrong, there were so many things of very great interest to see,
That we didn't have time to see everything there, my dearest beloved and me.

We did see..

Tractors, trailers, trucks and cars,
Fancy fruit cakes, jams in jars,
Horses, rabbits, dogs and cows,
Cavies, puppies, goats and fowls;
Shearers shearing sheep with ease,
Morris dancers, bells on knees;
Ferrets racing down some pipes,
Mowers, all of different types;
Axemen, too, of every age,
Country music on the stage;
Engines, hay rakes, chainsaws, pumps;
Camels, too, with saddled humps.
A shingle splitter splitting wood,
Showgirl entrants looking good;
Needlework of every sort,
Stalls where produce could be bought.

Children's craft and children's art,
Hardly knew just where to start!

Watched the Grand Parade, of course,
Saw a farrier shoe a horse.
Saw the rides and ferris wheel,
Listened to the youngsters squeal;
Saw the local gem display,
And the fashions of the day:
Listened to the Police Pipe Band,
Bought a cone at the ice cream stand;
Saw a vast array of flowers,
Stayed at the Show for sev'ral hours;
Saw a lot, but missed much more,
An early start next year, for sure!

RAGWORT

Ragwort, ragwort, wretched weed,
It's a plant we'll never need!
Been around for years and years,
Poisoning sheep, and calves and steers.

For farming stock, especially cattle,
Often fight a losing battle
If Ragwort features in their diet;
Ask a farmer - he won't deny it.

Controlled, but not eradicated,
Where the land is cultivated,
But is difficult to move
On paddocks steep or unimproved.

Sprays, of course, of various brands,
Help reduce the ragwort stands;
But farmers using this defence,
Find sprays incur a large expense.

But scientists, back in seventy-nine,
Made a most important find,
Introduced a tiny beetle,
To help control this weed a little.

Longitarsus flavicornis,
Whose appetite is quite enormous;
Significant control achieves
By eating ragwort's roots and leaves.

But control is now much greater,
For scientists, some nine years later;
Brought his Italian cousin here,
Longitarsus jacobaeae.

By making both these introductions
Ragwort's shown a huge reduction,
In areas where the beetle's sent,
Up to ninety-five per cent!

And so I'm glad for every farm
That suffers less from Ragwort's harm.
But the beetle that I need
Is one that eats each garden weed!

IT'S SPRING AGAIN

I have to write
A poem by tonight,
Tomorrow it's going to air.
But what can I say
In a poem today?
There's nought I can think of to share.

The sun is a-shining
But I am declining
To take the car out for a run.
Or relax in a chair
In the lovely fresh air,
For I've work inside to be done.

The snow on the hill
Remains with us still,
But winter is over and past.
I see, from my room,
The daffodils bloom,
And the robins are nesting, at last.

The wattles are best
If I look to the west,
A golden and glorious show.
And the ewes and the rams
Are surrounded by lambs,
In the fields in the valley below.

A sweet, gentle breeze
Caresses the trees,
And their leaves respond in delight.
But I'm out of luck,
For here I am stuck,
Wondering what I can write.

I hear the birds sing,
For now it is spring,
Outside is a cloudless blue sky.
But still I sit here,
My computer screen clear,
And time is a-hurrying by.

It's sad, but it's true,
No verse could I do,
At least I can say I have tried.
So bother the writing,
The sun's too inviting,
I'm joining the others outside.

A IS FOR APPLE

I was sitting in my library and from the shelf I took
A ninety-year old volume, a fruit culturist's book.
'Twas written in America; I've glanced at it before,
But, on this day, I searched the pages just a little more;
I read about diseases of leaf and bud and root,
And, near the back, varieties were listed for each fruit.
Much to my amazement, the apple list was great,
Two thousand sorts of apples were grown in the States!

A is for Ashton - it's tender and sweet,
B is for Boalsburg - a striped one to eat.
C is for Conway - it's most aromatic,
D is for Davis - it's colour dramatic!
E is for Epsy - it's handsome, but small,
F is for Forney, maturing late fall.
G is for Greenskin - it's rich and good-looking,
H is for Hilton - it's used just for cooking.
I is for Ingram - red fruit spotted white,
J is for Johnson - it's flesh a delight.
K is for Kelsey - it's yellowish-green,
L is for Landon - in winter it's seen.
M is for Minkler - it's conic and red,
N is for Nonsuch - great flavour, it's said.
O is for Orndorf - has excellent taste,
P is for Priestley - it's too good to waste.
Queen Anne is for Q - it's not very nice,
R's for Rebecca - a strong hint of spice.
S is for Stanard - it's large and it's round,
T is for Titus - best Russian around.
U is for Utter - a popular sort,
V is for Vermont - it's fruit's often bought.
W's Weston - it's pleasant and mild,
X the unknown one that grows in the wild.
Y is for Yacob, Z is for Zane,
That's all that you'll hear - I won't read it again!

ROVING STOCK

Every district has 'em, some loose and roving stock,
That tend to get on everybody's nerves,
It's not funny, I can tell you - they can give you quite a shock
When you meet them on some greasy mountain curves.

We've got a few at present, a mob of nine or ten,
That wander round our little country road;
Last month they were a nuisance, and now they're out again,
And the cattle's absent owner hasn't showed!

When it happened last September they were put into the pound,
But that's not such an easy thing to do;
For to yard them and to truck them's up to local folk around,
And the cost is shared by local people, too!

We like our front gate open, the one that's on the drive,
But now it's shut, and shut it has to stay;
And we're thankful that the gardens round the house are still alive,
For the roving stock got in the other day.

We managed to remove them ere they started on the plants,
But, just the same, it's not an easy job!
For the wretched frisky cattle led us both a merry dance!
They really are an irritating mob!

So all you farmers listening make sure your stock is safe;
Keep all your fences strained, and check your gates;
For if your stock is wandering on the roads around the place,
There's every chance you'll lose a lot of mates!

"LISTER'S SEPOYLE"

While staying on my nephew's farm I strolled into his shed;
He'd put a new roof on it, and "Take a look," he said.
So I gazed in admiration at each newly-painted truss,
And on his able handwork made the right amount of fuss.

Before I left his workshop I had a look around
At the many useful items on the bench and on the ground;
A compressor and an anvil, and some vises bolted fast,
And, set up in a corner, some bellows from the past.

On a shelf just near the window there were bottles, tins and jars,
With stuff for killing insects, mending leaks and greasing cars;
And a can of black and yellow that stood seven inches high,
And was labelled "Lister's Sepoyle" that the farmers used to buy.

I reached beside the window and I took the can outside,
For I couldn't read the writing, no matter how I tried;
But in the light I read the words - after brushing off the soil,
Lister's Sepoyle was the finest sort of separator oil.

A quarter gallon can it was, and sold by G and N,
Although I doubt you'll ever buy this type of oil again:
"Insure against all troubles, stiff bearings, gummed-up gears,"
The label, as I read it, took me back to earlier years.

When just a lad I'd visited my Aunt and Uncle's farm,
And watched as Auntie Margaret turned the separator's arm,
I wonder, now, if after she had done her daily toil,
She used Gippsland and Northern's finest Separator Oil!

FARM ANIMALS

Cows and horses, sheep and pigs, perhaps a goat or two,
Were what were kept upon a farm, as everybody knew;
There also were the dogs and cats, the ducks and geese and chooks,
And that was all the farmyard beasts that filled our picture books.

But that was in the olden days, back forty years and more,
Now farms around the country have surprises by the score!
We still can see the animals that farmers always raised,
But, if our granddad lived today, I think he'd be amazed!

Amazed, not only by TV, Computers and the like,
And air-conditioned tractors, and the four-wheeled motor-bike;
But old-timers would, I think, if from the past released,
Be most surprised at paddocks filled with many weird beasts.

Oh! the cows and horses, sheep and pigs they'd recognise all right,
But what about alpacas? They'd not know them by sight;
They would consider llamas strange, the ostrich they'd find queer;
Not to mention emu farms, or herds of fallow deer.

I wonder what we'll see on farms some forty years from now?
We'll still have sheep and cattle, and various types of fowl;
But will we farm the wallaby, or breed the kangaroo,
To bring us export dollars, or to put into our stew?

We might be raising wombats, or bandicoots and hares,
Or some exotic creatures like the elephant or bears;
Who knows? We may have farms of trees pointing to the sky,
To raise the local possum for the great Australian pie!

THE GALVANISED WATER TANK

After many years a galvanised tank will falter and start to leak,
For rust corrodes the iron sheets, and the bolted joints grow weak.
Although now failed as a water tank, it's rarely thrown away,
For the farmer knows that the rusted tank will live for many a day.

He disconnects all the pipes and taps and lifts it down from the stand,
And usually cuts the worst end out, avoiding slicing his hand.
By lying the empty tank on its side and putting it by the shed,
The tank he once used for water now stores his wood instead.

Not only for wood is it used to hold, it's also used for hay;
Or put in the paddock for stock to use on a cold and windy day.
Others are made quite comfortable with a few old sacks inside,
A perfect kennel for working dogs in which they can reside.

The farmer sometimes cuts the tank into two identical halves,
For these make excellent feeders for his sheep, his goats, and his calves.
I've also seen a cubby-house with a door and windows, too,
Made from a rusty water tank - when painted it looked like new.

I've no more time to tell you about the farmer's inventive ways,
Or support the galvanised water tank with further words of praise;
Sufficient to say to each of you, as you drive through our country green,
To observe the use of the rusty tanks and how clever the farmer's been!

THE HOUSE OF TRELOAR

At their farm I arrived
About quarter past five,
And that's when I first had misgivings.
I'd been offered some board,
And the rent could afford,
So accepted their bed with thanksgiving.

I'd not been there before,
And gasped as I saw
The filthiest yard I'd seen ever.
Mud, compost, manure,
Plus junk, made a sewer
Look like a fresh mountain river.

Through this unwholesome sludge
The farm animals trudged,
And the children played happily in it.
And there, at the door,
Stood the wife, Pat Treloar,
Calling out that she'd just be a minute.

She pulled on some boots,
Gave some guffawing hoots,
And tramped over, still roaring with laughter.
"Come in, luv!" she bawled,
So meekly I crawled
From my car, and stepped gingerly after.

When I ventured inside,
I very near died,
The smell in the house was appalling.
And the yard seemed to creep
Through the back door, and seep
Into each crack and chink in the flooring.

"Would you like cup o' tea?"
Pat bellowed at me,
And no reason I found for refusing.
From the teapot she drew
A foul-smelling brew,
That was not to my taste or my choosing.

As I sat with my drink,
Pat stood at the sink;
She prepared all the food as I eyed her.
All the peelings and skins,
All the bottles and tins,
She tossed through the window beside her.

Soon after being fed
I went off to bed,
Away from the rubbish disgusting.
'Twas an old wooden bunk;
And the room, full of junk,
Could have done with a clean and a dusting.

But the air was less rank,
And, though it smelt dank,
The room was both peaceful and quiet.
And the bed, although old,
Proved to keep out the cold,
Once I pulled back the covers to try it.

Not feeling too bright,
I switched off the light,
And tried to forget what I'd eaten.
For our dinner had been
A stew, most obscene;
My stomach, though tough, was near beaten.

I was hoping to sleep;
Have a rest, long and deep,
But this was a hope soon exploded.
Once the room became black,
There emerged from a crack
Some beasts, and my peace was eroded.

As they scurried nearby,
I decided to lie
In the dark, and try to ignore them.
But of this was no chance,
For they made an advance
On the bed-posts, and started to gnaw them.

The noise was so great,
I became most irate,
And I turned on the light to deter them.
But they steadily sat,
Those abominable rats;
I was greatly repulsed by these vermin.

I ran quickly outside,
For some fresh air I cried;
But, alas, the air was polluted.
What with pig sties nearby,
Rotting cabbage piled high,
My stomach felt most convoluted.

My distress was intense
As I leaned on the fence,
And my stomach gave in altogether.
But, at last, I returned
To the bedroom, and yearned
To be gone from this farmhouse for ever.

I survived there a week,
But my future looked bleak,
Had I stayed in that house any longer.
I'd enough of the rats,
And the squalling of brats,
And the smell which grew steadily stronger.

So I made some excuse
To this family obtuse,

And drove to my home in the city.
I soaked in the bath
For an hour and a half,
To get rid of the stench and self-pity!

I was able to find
Board of different kind,
And very happy I was, to be sure.
And I now seldom speak
Of that horrible week
I endured in the house of Treloar.

A PENNY A PAN

A penny a pan was the going rate, if my memory serves me right,
It might have been double at twopence a pan, but I'd rather the cart at night;
But the Council charge was a half-a-crown which was far too much to ask,
So the teacher's job in the one-man school included this weekly task.

Not only a nineteenth century task, for the teacher performed this chore
In many Victorian Government schools until nineteen sixty four:
I know this is true for I taught in those schools, and in weather both hot or cold,
After lunch every Friday afternoon I'd be out there digging a hole.

In summer when the ground dried out a shovel just wasn't enough,
One also needed a mattock or pick, e'en then the going was tough;
But winter and rain made a quagmire again, and the black soil turned to glue,
And to dig a hole with the ground like that was a terrible job to do.

While the teacher was out a-digging a hole, the children were all inside,
Happily tearing the place apart, if the noise was any guide.
Once the hole was dug the teacher would call for the strongest grade six lad,
And together they'd go, both holding their nose, for, I tell you, the smell was bad!

Carefully lifting the heavy pan with load, they'd struggle across to the pit,
And gingerly empty the contents in, and hoped that it all would fit.
When the second pan had been emptied too, there was little more to face,
Just fill in the hole, disinfect the pans, and return them both to their place.

A penny a pan was the going rate, and whether for duty or love,
Or necessity, or the vegies that grew so well on the ground above,
One thing is for sure - and I swear this is true - I wouldn't lie or be funny,
The teacher whose round included this task never did it for the money!

COUNTRY COOKING

Roast lamb, baked potatoes and peas mother fed us;
Or steak with three vegies (including some greens);
Or p'raps some cold meat with tomatoes and lettuce;
Or rissoles, hamburgers, with pumpkin and beans.

This orderly diet was what I was used to,
For twenty-three years I had eaten such fare:
Now up country to teach I'd been sent (didn't choose to);
I felt some anxiety travelling there.

I stayed with a widow who fed me like mother,
(Roast lamb, baked potatoes, and peas with mint sauce),
The meals that she cooked me were much like each other,
Plain country-style cooking - I ate like a horse!

But to tea I was asked by Pat and Pete Turner,
And, out of politeness, accepted, of course,
And trusted that Pat as a cook was no learner,
(Roast lamb, baked potatoes, and peas with mint sauce).

I drove to their farm and was welcomed most warmly,
They offered me goat's milk with celery and cheese;
'Twas then that I said to myself most forlornly,
"No hope of roast dinner with mint sauce and peas."

For tea we had coleslaw and other raw foodstuff,
Like carrot, tomato, rice salad, and beet,
With side serves of bean shoots, alfalfa, and peanuts,
"Goodbye baked potato, green peas, and roast meat."

After eating a meal of food unrewarding,
I left after drinking a cup of herb tea.
I drove back to Williams' - that's where I was boarding,
And found that my mother had telephoned me.

I rang her straightway, for her health I had doubted;
She said, "I just rang to give you a choice
Of what meals you would like at the weekend." - I shouted,
"Roast lamb, baked potatoes and peas with mint sauce!"

THE POSSUM CATCHER

He had finished Teachers' College,
And his head was full of knowledge,
But it wasn't quite sufficient for what now had come about.
All his higher education
Did not help the situation,
He'd a possum in the chimney and he couldn't get it out.

For the bulk of his existence
He'd been very little distance
From the borders of the city and the comforts that it brought.
Now he was a country teacher,
And could hear the wretched creature
Scrabbling in the bricked up chimney where 'twas obviously caught.

No Psychology or History
Was a help. It was a mystery
How a possum could be rescued from behind a bricked-up hearth.
Late at night and early morning,
Both his wife and he woke, yawning,
As the possum, scratching loudly, sought to find an exit path.

"I'm sure the possum's weaker,"
'Twas his wife who was the speaker;
To her husband she was talking as he came home late from school.
Well, the thought of possum lying
In the chimney, then expiring,
Was too much for both these people, it seemed pitiful and cruel.

"We must save him, that is certain,
Ere he rings the final curtain."
But 'twas not for noble reasons that the rescue would be made.
For the thought of odours rotten
Coming from the chimney bottom,
Was enough to see that rescue plans would not be long delayed.

So the problem that existed
Had no answer that was listed
In a College course, or covered by a Bachelor's Degree.
So with all his mental vigour,
The schoolteacher tried to figure
How to move that curs-ed possum from the chimney to a tree.

But no answer was forthcoming,
And it sounded like the drumming
Of the possum in the chimney was much weaker to the ear.
"I'll just have to up and feed him,
For we cannot really leave him;
And I'll ask the local farmers how to get him out of here."

Now it happened that a neighbour,
Looking upward from his labour,
Saw the teacher silhouetted on the schoolhouse roof next door.
He was hanging, rather grimly,
By his right hand, to the chimney:
The astonished neighbour waited just to see what was in store.

So the neighbour watched intently,
As the teacher, very gently,
Began dropping bits of bread and fruit straight down the chimney black.
Then he carefully descended
From the roof-top, and intended
To go inside the schoolhouse, but the neighbour called him back.

So the poor, embarrassed teacher
Told the story of the creature
Trapped in the bricked-up fireplace behind their bedroom wall.
The neighbour said, with eyes a-twinkle,
"You need a fishing-line to winkle
Out that possum from the chimney if it's had a nasty fall."

Not approving this suggestion,
The schoolteacher went to question
All the farmers in the district how to set the possum free.
"Fill the chimney up with water,
Shouldn't hurt the bricks and mortar;
Then the possum, floating upwards, can be put into a tree."

"Drop a rope so he can grab it."
"Set a trap like for a rabbit,
Tie it on a piece of string and catch him in its iron teeth."
"Get a piece of fencing wire,
(Number eight, but nothing higher),
Long enough to reach the possum in the chimney underneath.

Spin it round and round quite quickly,
Since the possum's feeling sickly,
It won't move, and you will catch it when the wire sticks in its fur."
"Take a ferret and attach it
To a string, and he will catch it."
"Knock the bricks out and extract him, then replace them as they were."

Now the teacher, with his problem,
Had the mickey taken from him;
And he knew it, but the possum was still trapped behind the bricks.
When he reached home, night was falling,
And he heard his partner calling,
"The possum's on the roof-top and he's heading for the sticks!"

Now the teacher, disbelieving
That the possum now was leaving,
Climbed up onto the housetop just as fast as he could race.
But the possum was much quicker,
He could almost hear it snicker
As it, diving down the chimney, grinned back up at teacher's face.

It could scamper up the chimney
Very easily, very nimbly;
And the teacher, red-faced, panting, tried to grab it by the tail.
But the possum kept retreating,
And the teacher's loud entreating
Could not entice the possum from inside its so-called gaol.

It was getting close to midnight
When the teacher, in the moonlight,
Climbed up onto the roof again armed with a concrete block.
On the chimney he then set it,
And the possum, when he met it,
Knew the chimney now was sealed with a very heavy lock.

But this saga had not finished,
For the interest, undiminished,
In the story by the locals went for ever on and on.
And for many months thereafter,
With their faces creased with laughter,
They would ask the blushing teacher had his possum problem gone!

THE TAIL OF A SNAKE

They used to ride to school each day,
Each on their horse, from miles away:
The Barton kids, I can't recall
Their Christian names at all, at all.
Two boys, one girl, (I think that's right),
They were a most familiar sight
Out on that Western District road
That led to school from their abode.
In weather fine or weather vile,
They'd ride to school in single file.

On reaching school each horse was led
Around behind the shelter shed,
And through the 'pony paddock' gate.
And then, with saddles off, they'd wait
Throughout the day till school was out,
When all the children, with a shout,
Would tumble from the schoolroom door.
They'd saddle up each horse before
Riding down that road again,
In wind, or sun, or driving rain.

Now it so happened that the yard
That kept the horses safely barred,
Lay 'twixt the teacher's house and school.
And I, at lunchtime, as a rule,
Would walk across that yard to greet
My wife, and have some food to eat.
I'd pass the saddles in a row,
And through the gate to home I'd go.
One day, when I'd two saddles passed,
I saw a tail beneath the last.

Now, even 'though my background lay
In city streets and buildings grey,,
I knew that saddles don't grow tails,
(At least, not brown ones made of scales).
I stopped. I thought. I thought some more.
The problem was not what I saw.
The problem was, it seemed to me,
Was that part which I couldn't see.
I couldn't go and leave the snake,
That left a risk too big to take.
I pondered on what I should do.
I thought the problem through and through.
Eventually I called for Joe
To bring to me the garden hoe.
I, to the other children said,
"All stand beside the shelter shed."
When the hoe was in my hand,
I went ahead with what I'd planned;
And hoping that I would not fail,
I jammed the hoe down on that tail!

Then, with a stick that lay nearby,
I raised the Barton's saddle high:
But then I saw I had not won,
My troubles now had just begun.
For, though I now had trapped the tail,
The other end, with much travail,
Had gone, as far as hoe would let,
Had gone, as far as it could get,
Had ventured down (not all, but most)
A hole beside the strainer post.

The children, wide-eyed, watched with glee,
As there, transfixed with snake, was me.
To loose the hoe would give the snake
Far better than an even break.
To hold the hoe, I had to stay,
Like Peter and the dyke, all day!
To overcome this impasse, I
Had one more option I could try:
With heart in mouth and features pale,
I wrapped my hand around that tail!

The thought I had behind this act
Was that I could this beast extract
From whence it lay, and then to break
The neck of this confounded snake.
And so I pulled - to no avail,
The snake held tight - I held the tail.
I pulled and pulled, but all in vain,
The snake was equal to the strain.
At last I tugged with all my might,
And threw the snake away in fright.

The snake, by now with temper high,
Turned to attack, and so did I!
I swung the hoe and gave a shout
And knocked snake down, but not right out.
The snake reared up and danced and struck,
But I, with just an ounce of luck,
Struck snake once more, this time for good,
And killed him with a piece of wood.
The children, now the show had ceased,
Returned to play their games in peace.

And I, retreating to the house,
Was calmed by sympathetic spouse.
Extending lunch by half an hour,
I took a nerve-restoring shower.
I walked the long way back to school,
And reinforced the playground rule
Regarding snakes. The Barton's said
They'd keep their horse gear in the shed.
I hope again I'll never see
A tailed saddle next to me!

PETER

A weak chest they'd have called it in grandmother's day,
For he caught every cold that happened his way;
Along with bronchitis, pneumonia and 'flu;
And, to make matters worse, he was asthmatic, too.

Tough little Peter took these in his stride,
But that wasn't all that he had to abide.
As if all his ills weren't enough to go through,
Cerebral palsy afflicted him too.

With irons on his legs he managed to stand,
But to walk anywhere he held someone's hand.
But, in spite of his ailments, this brave little lad
Was as cheerful a pupil as I've ever had.

To go to the Spastic Society's school,
He'd have had to leave home, a circumstance cruel.
His Dad and Mum asked me, "Can you think of a way,
That Peter can come to our school every day?"

For disabled children there was no support
In schools where students were normally taught;
There were some Special Schools, but only a few,
And, like the Society's School, were a great distance too.

So I said to his parents that Peter could start
At our one-teacher school, and they, on their part,
Must see that their son was able to cope
With eating,and toiletting, washing and soap!

'Twas Judy, his sister, who helped him each day,
She fed him and washed him, and took him to play;
Inside he struggled when moving around,
But outside on his trike he raced over the ground!

He soon proved a favourite, this brave little chap,
Who fought every day his severe handicap.
The others involved him in all of their fun;
From the oldest Grade Six to the youngest Grade One.

As a student he shone, he was good with his head,
Although we had trouble with much that he said.
For his speech was affected, and it took us some time
To make of his chatter any reason or rhyme!

Throughout second term he was often away,
For his health couldn't cope with the chill winter days;
With Springtime, however, young Peter returned
Determined as ever, and anxious to learn.

But, despite the tremendous strength of his will,
Peter's health, to our sorrow, continued downhill;
Through summer and autumn he battled and fought
Each asthma attack, each infection he caught.

At the end of the autumn his schooldays were past,
For the following winter was young Peter's last;
His ills that for years he'd boldly defied,
Overcame him at last, and the little boy died.

The whole district was saddened by Peter's demise;
And his little white coffin brought tears to all eyes.
Although this young death was enormously sad,
To have been Peter's teacher I'm eternally glad.

ONCE BITTEN.....

I was going round the classroom warning all the children there
To take certain wise precautions in the summer, and beware
Of dangerous Gippsland creatures; I had some samples, too,
Jars of spiders, biting insects, and a black snake frozen through.

A farmer brought the snake to me, he'd killed it on his farm;
'Twas every inch of five feet long and thick as my right arm.
I coiled the snake up carefully, and, wrapped in plastic clear,
I placed it in the freezer, where I left it for a year.

My wife, although a patient soul, ultimately said,
"You've had the snake for long enough, it's over twelve months dead.

Get rid of it, my freezer is for keeping food, not snakes."
And so I took it to the school, for all the children's sakes.

To make the lessons int'resting, I showed to every class
The frozen snake, and passed around the creatures kept in glass.
I had a blue-tongued lizard too, Telequa was its name;
It was alive, and lived at school, and was completely tame.

The lessons were a great success, but, just like anything,
The snake would partially defrost, extending like a spring.
Its head I'd hook across my thumb, the body would hang down,
And then the blue-tongued lizard would sit up on its crown.

I'd take the load from class to class and, when there was a break,
I'd go back to the staff-room 'fridge to freeze the thawing snake.
It was as I was walking down the passage from Room Five,
Two sixth grade boys called out to me, "That snake, is it alive?"

I reassured them that the snake was well and truly dead;
But that was when Telequa chose to move his scaly head.
One boy exclaimed, "His head just moved!" and, continuing to come,
He knocked my hand; the snake's head slipped, and fangs dug in my thumb!

Now, even 'though the snake was dead and frozen through and through,
Its poison still was in the fangs, and therefore in me too!
I washed the wound as best I could, but it was then too late;
My thumb for days was sore and red - I didn't feel too great!

And so my warnings dire and grim were justified completely,
The lessons gained new int'rest, and the wound healed up quite neatly.
But truth, they say, is stranger than the things you may have read -
The only snake that's bitten me had been for twelve months dead!

MARBLES

A giant of enormous size, a huge colossus without peer,
Once, strolling through this block of land, played marbles with the boulders here.
I think he was a teenage giant, an adolescent titan pup,
For he, on finishing his game, made no attempt to pick them up.

THE DISTRICT INSPECTOR

The District Inspector was very much feared,
His powerful position was almost revered,
And teachers would tremble whenever he neared,
To make an inspection.
Some District Inspectors were gentle enough,
But most seem constructed of much sterner stuff,
A few were discourteous, their manner was gruff
On days of inspection.

The District Inspector would come without warning,
Sometimes after midday, but usually morning,
The day would pass slowly, but don't be seen yawning!
On days of inspection.

Work Programmes he'd read with a critical eye,
And errors in Courses he couldn't pass by,
And some teachers felt that they'd rather die,
Than face an inspection!

CITY VISITORS

We had shifted to the country only eighty miles from town,
To a pleasant little schoolhouse, and there we settled down;
Our relatives and friends were glad to come and visit there,
To stay a while; a day, a week; then back to town repair.

Most visitors who came to stop would really pull their weight,
By drying dishes, cleaning up, and not staying up too late.
And we were glad to see them, but as winter blustered in,
The joy of constant relatives was wearing rather thin!

Brother, sister, cousin, niece, acquaintance, aunt, or friend;
More than half a year had gone without a free weekend.
And then a fellow came to stay, and brought along his tribe;
His manners were deplorable; his speech I won't describe.

He left his children in our care, or left them for his wife
To deal with petty discipline, attend to any strife.
He claimed the best seat by the fire, he never helped at all;
He'd read the papers first each day, then drop them in the hall.

No conversation could be held but that he'd dominate,
He'd voice his views in strident tone with ill-informed debate.
When he'd been there for seven days, he'd still a week to go,
Not since we'd left the city had the time gone past so slow!

....

To pump the water for the house (for me, a daily chore),
I'd have to pump by hand each night for half-an-hour, or more.
The four-foot handle on the pump, I'd push it to and fro
To fill the tank up on the roof, and make the water flow.

Most visitors who came to stay would offer to assist,
And usually their offer I would courteously resist;
But Jim, he asked me why each night I pumped for half-an-hour;
I spoke, and none too gently said,"I'm pumping up YOUR shower!"

His short reply was to the point, I still can hear him say,
"There's not a chance of me doing that, I'm here on holiday!"
'Twas fortunate for Jim that day the handle was not loose,
He might have suffered greatly from some physical abuse!

We suffered Jim a few more days, and then he left for town;
I think by then he understood the "WELCOME" sign was down.
His children now have all grown up; they often come to stay;
But Jim, he's got the message, for he's kept himself away!

FLIES

Our God, all-wise
Created flies,
But gave no explanation,
Why flies that crawl
Upon us all
Are needed in our nation!

POOR MARY

They lived in the scrub several miles from the school,
And both arrived late as a general rule;
"Hillbilly's" the word that suited them best -
They were certainly different from all of the rest.

These two little children the same mother had,
But no-one was certain just who was their dad!
For their farm was the home to a number of folk,
And the butt, unrequested, of many a joke.

Andrew was eight, and his sister was five,
A scrap of humanity barely alive;
With blonde hair like straw, and a badly-turned eye.
On her first day at school she was ready to cry.

We welcomed them both, and settled her down,
But were unable to rid her face of its frown:
I gave her a pencil, and suggested she draw,
But she had no idea what a pencil was for!

I told her to hold it, and showed her the lead,
And how, on the paper, the marks came out red.
She sat there bemused, but, after a while,
She scribbled away, and e'en cracked a smile!

A few minutes later she stood by my side,
And held up the pencil and very near cried.
'Twas easy to see that she'd broken the lead;
"My pencil is buggered," this tiny tot said.

For three years I taught her - I'm happy to tell,
Although starting badly, she fitted in well.
She was happy at school, and learnt with the rest,
But I couldn't say truthfully that she was the best.

After leaving the school I rather lost touch
With this sister and brother, and didn't hear much.
But several years later, I was sorry to glean,
This poor little lass was a mum at fifteen.

GARDENING

I was told that one should exercise 'bout every second day,
And this would keep the rolls of fat and heart disease away.
I sought to find a hobby that would keep me fit and trim,
With not too strenuous labour, nor risking life and limb.

Energetic sports were out, aerobics and the like;
And I wasn't keen sailing, or riding on my bike;
So I settled then for gardening, it seemed to fill the bill;
A little daily exercise, and is rarely known to kill!

So I started on the garden, if that's what you could call
An untidy yard of grass and dirt that stretched from fence to wall.
I tackled it undaunted, I knew I'd have it done
In just a month or two of work - it even might be fun!

It's now a year later, my forecast proved me wrong,
I'm quite amazed that such a job has taken me so long!
And exercise! You'd never guess what labour I've put in;
I've lost a dozen kilograms, and now look pretty thin.

> I've weeded and seeded, I've planted and mowed,
> I've lifted and shifted, I'ver panted and blowed.
> I've cut edges and hedges, I've poisoned and sprayed;
> Dishevelled, I've levelled, and bricks I have laid.
> With mixtures and fixtures and cost I have potted,
> With soil and with toil compost I have rotted;
> I've raked and I've staked, and holes I have dug,
> And, at war every day, I have fought every bug!

And now I'm very tired, my garden's barely tidy,
Seven days a week I've worked, from Saturday to Friday.
I haven't now the energy to work my garden bed,
I'm off to play a lesser sport - I'll swim and run instead!

RAIN

It's rained in Nunamara, it's rained in Hobart Town;
Right throughout Tasmania the rain has tumbled down.
The hikers and the campers were drenched on Freycinet,
And it's almost unbelievable the rain they've had at Gray!
With creeks and rivers flooding all around the State,
It's only now the Bureau says the rain may soon abate.
From Saturday till Wednesday it never ceased to drop,
Causing mudslides on the highways, and making traffic stop.
I think this time the Rain Gods took their joke a bit too far;
All I did was plan a barbecue, and carefully washed the car!

DEATH OF A GIANT

I found a fallen giant today,
What caused its death I cannot say:
Old age? The wind? White ants, or rot?
Whate'er the cause, it matters not.
For centuries, maybe, it had grown,
And not a sign of weakness shown.
It had withstood the heat and frost,
And, when the winter tempest tossed
Its fiercest storm, the tree had stood
Unbowed, as mighty giants should.
But now its dead. Its broken back
Forlornly lies across our track.
Last afternoon it filled the sky,
But now upon the ground will lie
Subject to gradual decay.
Farewell, O giant of yesterday !